5/01

Teen Pregnancy

Tough Choices

By Julie K. Endersbe, MEd

Consultant:
Jennifer A. Oliphant, MPH
Research Fellow and Community Outreach Coordinator
National Teen Pregnancy Prevention Research Center
Division of General Pediatrics and Adolescent Health
University of Minnesota

Perspectives on Healthy Sexuality

LifeMatters
an imprint of Capstone Press
Mankato, Minnesota

LifeMatters books are published by Capstone Press
818 North Willow Street • Mankato, Minnesota 56001
http://www.capstone-press.com

Printed in the United States of America

Library of Congress Cataloging-in-Publication Data
Endersbe, Julie.
      Teen pregnancy : tough choices / by Julie Endersbe.
         p.   cm. — (Perspectives on healthy sexuality)
      Includes bibliographical references and index.
      Summary: Describes what teenagers can expect during and after pregnancy, the options to abort, choose adoption, or become a parent, methods of preventing pregnancy, and other dilemmas and solutions.
      ISBN 0-7368-0271-1 (book). — ISBN 0-7368-0293-2 (series)
      1. Teenage parents—United States—Juvenile literature. 2. Teenage pregnancy—United States—Juvenile literature. [1. Pregnancy. 2. Teenage parents. 3. Sex instruction for youth.] I. Title. II. Series: Endersbe, Julie. Perspectives on healthy sexuality.
      HQ759.64 .E53 2000
      306.874´3—dc21   99-29801
                          CIP

Staff Credits
Anne Heller, editor; Adam Lazar, designer; Heidi Schoof, photo researcher

Photo Credits
Cover: ©FPG International/Bill Losh
FPG International/©Telegraph Colour Library, 7; ©James Levin, 18; ©Barbara Peacock, 20; ©Michael Hart, 39; ©Jim Whitmer, 47; ©Mark Harmel, 48
Photobank, Inc./©Skjold, 24, 34; ©Carmen Northen, 42
International Stock Photo/©Stan Pak, 33; ©George Ancona, 59
Unicorn Stock Photos/©Tom McCarthy, 9; ©Eric R. Berndt, 14; ©Deneve Bunde, 30; ©Richard B. Dippold, 32; ©Jeff Greenberg, 56
Uniphoto Picture Agency/27, 55; ©Bob Daemmrich, 57

A 0 9 8 7 6 5 4 3 2 1

Table of Contents

Chapter Overview

Females begin menstruating around age 12 but may not marry until around age 25. A female teen's body is ready to reproduce, but she and her partner may not be ready to parent.

The rate of sexual activity among teens today is high. Sexual activity involves the possibilities of pregnancy and sexually transmitted diseases.

Half of all teen pregnancies occur within six months after the female first begins having intercourse.

Chapter 1

The Issues of Teen Pregnancy

Gerald was really special. We did
everything together. He would pick me up

Tina, Age 17

before school and walk me to my classes. We usually went to
my house after school. My mom's never home. I didn't think
I'd have sex until I was older, but it didn't turn out that way. I
wanted my first time to be with someone special. I thought
Gerald would be with me forever.

I didn't want to get pregnant, so I asked Gerald to go buy some
condoms. He bought them, but things happened so fast that we
didn't use them. I got pregnant right away. When I told Gerald
about the pregnancy, he seemed to freeze. He doesn't call
anymore. I'm too young to have a baby. I feel so alone.

Many adolescents begin having intercourse about eight years before they marry.

While the likelihood of having intercourse increases steadily with age, one in five people do not have intercourse during their teens.

Many people believe teen pregnancy is a social crisis. They think that the teen pregnancy rate is the worst it has ever been. It is true that the teen pregnancy rate is higher in the United States than in other developed countries. The fact is, however, that the birth rate among U.S. teens declined in the 1990s. Between 1990 and 1996, the rate of teen pregnancy dropped 17 percent.

A teen couple who are going to have a baby may feel like they are in crisis. They have to make a choice among parenthood, adoption, or abortion.

The Issue of Teen Pregnancy

The average age of marriage today is 25. The average girl begins menstruating around age 12. That means she might not marry for another 10 years or longer. Even so, her hormone levels are high, and her body is ready to reproduce. Her body is functioning as it should be. Yet a 12-year-old girl isn't ready to be a mother.

Today teens face many challenges. For example, many teens are sexually active. By age 18, 56 percent of girls and 73 percent of boys are sexually active. Unplanned pregnancies can happen when teens choose to be sexually active. In the United States, most people become sexually active about eight years before marriage.

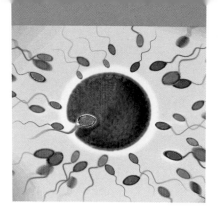

I thought all my friends were having **Lawrence, Age 16** sex. They were always talking about sex and all. I had been dating Laticia for almost a year. She had "slept" with her last boyfriend. I really liked her a lot. She said she was on birth control pills and that it was safe and all. We had sexual intercourse on our one-year anniversary.

I really had something for Laticia. I didn't know she was messing with my mind. I should have known that she never used the pill. She wanted to have a baby with me, so she got pregnant. Now I feel betrayed. I should have taken more responsibility. I could have worn a condom. At least I would have been protecting myself.

The Results of Sexual Activity

There is always a possibility that sexual activity will result in pregnancy or a sexually transmitted disease (STD). Conception, or pregnancy, is a result of a male's sperm fertilizing a female's egg. This happens during sexual intercourse. When a male ejaculates sperm inside or near a female's vagina, she can become pregnant. Half of all adolescent pregnancies happen within six months after the female first has intercourse. Twenty percent of pregnancies occur within the first month after a female first begins having intercourse.

"My friends think my daughter is so cute. They love to hold her and feed her. I keep telling them to wait. I love my daughter and can't imagine living without her, but there are definitely things I would choose to do differently. If you have a choice, WAIT! Don't get pregnant in your teens."
—Holly, age 17

More teens are using pregnancy prevention methods. Pregnancy can still happen, however, even when such methods are used.

Why Are Teens Getting Pregnant?

Each teen pregnancy happens for a different reason. Some teens choose to be sexually active because they think it is a way to show their love. They don't think about consequences such as pregnancy. Most teen pregnancies are not planned. Some teens choose to get pregnant. Others think a pregnancy would give them freedom such as moving out of their parents' home. Some young males may think making their girlfriend pregnant proves their manhood. Some young men want to pass on their family name.

The Influence of the Media

Some experts believe the media has influenced sexual activity among teens. Television, magazines, movies, musicians, and music videos all promote different ideas about sexuality. Teens must deal with mixed messages constantly.

Chapter Overview

Women may have signs or feelings they are pregnant. A woman should have a test at a clinic or hospital to confirm the pregnancy.

Pregnancy has three stages or trimesters. Each stage lasts about three months.

Childbirth can occur in two ways. In a vaginal birth, a baby is pushed out through the cervix and the vagina. A cesarean birth involves surgery.

Television complicates how a teen views sexuality. In fact, many teens spend more time watching television than they do in school. One study found that in a single year, more than 20,000 sexual messages were aired. These messages rarely promote protected sex or postponing sex until teens are older. Also, messages about pregnancy and disease prevention are seldom on television.

Points to Consider

Do you think pregnancy is a social crisis? Why or why not?

What do you think are some reasons that teens get pregnant?

Describe how the media might influence how teens feel about having sex.

What messages does the media give about being a female? How do the messages differ from those about being a male?

Chapter 2

What to Expect if You Are Pregnant

My girlfriend and I were going to get married after we graduated from high school. We had talked about our future and how many kids we wanted to have. But we were just talking. When we found out we were pregnant, we were shocked. I know we hadn't always been very careful, but you never think it's going to happen to you.

Felipe, Age 18

We talked mostly with our parents about the decision. They gave us so much support. Her mother said she could watch the baby while we finished school. My dad helped find me a part-time job. We decided we could make it work. We have good people around us. We know parenting will be hard work, but I feel better knowing we are working hard to become good parents.

A healthy lifestyle improves the chances of having a healthy baby. A pregnant woman should:

- Exercise regularly
- Eat healthy foods
- Consume caffeine in moderation
- Visit the doctor regularly
- Check with a doctor before taking any medicines
- Quit smoking or cut down on smoking as much as possible
- Not drink alcohol
- Not use any addicting drugs, including cocaine, marijuana, crack, or speed
- Learn healthy ways to relax and relieve stress

Early Signs of Pregnancy

Women who are pregnant notice certain body changes. They may feel more tired than usual. Some have an upset stomach. Their period is absent, late, or very light and spotty. Most women's breasts are swollen and tender. These are signs that women should check for pregnancy.

Many teens check for pregnancy by using a home pregnancy test. It is a quick, affordable way to confirm a pregnancy. Following the directions is important. If the test result is positive, an appointment should be made with a doctor. The doctor will do another pregnancy test to confirm, or make sure of, the pregnancy.

Stages of Pregnancy

Pregnancy has three stages. Each stage, or trimester, is about three months long. A woman usually delivers a baby in the third trimester between 38 and 42 weeks.

During the entire pregnancy, prenatal care is important for the health of the fetus and the mother. These doctor visits before a birth help prepare the mother and fetus for birth. The schedule for prenatal care visits is based on the development of the pregnancy.

A recommended schedule for prenatal visits during pregnancy

8 weeks pregnant	First appointment
8–35 weeks pregnant	Every 4 weeks
36–38 weeks pregnant	Every 2 weeks
39 or more weeks pregnant	Weekly until birth

Trimester I: 1 to 12 Weeks

The first trimester is the first three months of pregnancy. Many women experience morning sickness, or an upset stomach and vomiting. This problem often but not always happens in the morning. Only a few women with morning sickness have severe upset stomach or vomiting.

Women who choose to stay pregnant complete a health evaluation. The doctor asks questions about drug and alcohol use. Other questions concern sexual history, diet, and occupational hazards. It is important to answer these questions honestly. A woman's health history gives the doctor information about possible risks to the fetus.

Many tests are completed during the first trimester. Pregnant women may be tested for HIV, the virus that causes AIDS, and for other STDs.

Trimester II: 13 to 27 Weeks

The second trimester of pregnancy is often the most enjoyable. Most feelings of morning sickness decrease, and the tired feeling fades. The abdomen starts to enlarge. As the fetus grows, fetal movement may occur after 16 weeks. Usually a woman feels the movements by 20 weeks. Some women have headaches or a faint or dizzy feeling during this trimester.

Trimester III: 29 Weeks to Delivery

The body goes through large changes in the last trimester of pregnancy. The hips widen to prepare for birth. The breasts enlarge to prepare for feeding the baby. Physical discomfort increases as the baby grows. Backaches are more common. The pressure on the bladder makes urination more frequent.

The largest weight gain happens in the third trimester as the baby grows quickly. Normal weight gain during pregnancy is between 25 and 35 pounds. Young women who gain fewer than 20 pounds may put their baby at risk. Babies who weigh too little at birth may be more likely to have developmental problems.

Childbirth

The way in which a baby leaves its mother's uterus and is born is called labor, or childbirth. The length of labor varies with each woman. The average time is 12 to 15 hours for a first baby. The time can be much shorter or longer than this, however.

Babies are born in two ways. The most common way is vaginal birth. The woman pushes the baby out of her uterus. The baby then moves through the cervix, or opening to the uterus, and into the vagina. Each contraction, or tightening of the uterus, helps the baby move along. Many women receive medication to ease the pain of childbirth.

A vaginal birth usually has a short recovery period. The nurses at the hospital massage the abdomen to help it shrink. The new family usually goes home within 48 hours of the birth.

Teen Pregnancy

The other way a baby is born is cesarean section. This is done in an operating room. The woman receives a strong pain medicine. The doctor cuts through the abdominal wall and uterus. The mother cannot feel anything on the lower half of her body. She can be awake during the surgery.

A cesarean birth has a longer recovery period than vaginal birth does. It is major surgery. Mothers cannot lift heavy objects for several weeks. They are not even supposed to lift the baby. They need a lot of help around home. A mother should do very little during her recovery.

Preparing for a Baby

A teen couple can do many things to promote a healthy pregnancy and childbirth. Together, they can take childbirth classes. The father can go with the mother to prenatal doctor visits. They can enroll in a parenting or family living class at school. Such classes prepare them to be parents.

Teens who choose to parent must prepare themselves. Parenting is hard work. Babies need parents who are gentle and know how to care for them.

Points to Consider

What are some signs of a possible pregnancy?

Why is it important to learn the health history of a pregnant woman?

What are the two types of childbirth?

How can a teen father be involved during pregnancy and childbirth?

Chapter Overview

Having a baby can be exciting. At the same time, it is important to realize the difficulties of raising a child.

Babies have many needs. Diapering, feeding, and sleeping can be opportunities for parents to build an attachment with their baby.

Raising babies is expensive and takes up a lot of time.

Teens who are not married can establish paternity. This allows the child to have a legal father. The parent who does not have custody of a child usually pays child support.

Teen parents can work together to raise a baby. They can share responsibilities while each is attending school or work.

Chapter 3

What to Expect if You Choose Parenting

Romantic Images of Mothering

Friends may think a baby is cute and also want to have one. They may not realize how hard it is to be a parent. It's hard to find a good baby-sitter. It's hard to buy groceries. It's hard living at home with parents while raising the baby. Some teen mothers don't get a lot of help from the baby's father.

Teens who choose to raise a baby face many challenges. Babies are unpredictable. They get sick. They have immediate needs. Babies need a stable home where they can sleep in a quiet place. Most importantly, babies need to develop a warm attachment to their parents.

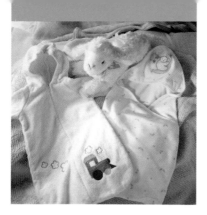

When Angela and I brought Savada home from the hospital, we were more than scared. **José, Age 19**
We didn't know what to do with a newborn. Luckily, my mom stayed with us for a week. We had taken childbirth and parenting classes. But we practiced with dolls. We never had the real thing!

Savada was a pretty good baby. She had her days and nights mixed up. It was hard for me to stay awake at school. Angela was home from school for the first month. She mostly got up nights. It was still hard for me to sleep. I would do the feedings on the weekends so Angela could sleep.

We are working hard to make it work. Angela and I sometimes fight. I think that once we get more sleep, it will be better. Angela and I wanted to have kids, but we thought it would be in five years. The pregnancy really changed our plans.

Care

There are many opportunities to build a healthy attachment between parents and baby. Teen parents can learn how to make the most of feeding time. The daily task of feeding can be made enjoyable for a baby. Parents who hold their baby close and talk to the child build a connection. This warm interaction can occur during any time that is spent with the child.

Babies need to visit the doctor regularly. Early visits to the doctor ensure that the baby is healthy. The doctor monitors the baby's growth. The baby receives immunizations or vaccinations. These shots keep the baby safe from childhood diseases.

Expenses

Babies are expensive. The birth alone can cost thousands of dollars. Most young women are covered under their parents' health insurance. Finding affordable health insurance can be a major task. Studies show babies who are covered with good health insurance tend to be healthier.

Other expenses include furniture, clothes, and diapers. Many parents choose to buy second-hand furniture and clothes. Babies rarely wear anything out because they sleep most of the time. Used cribs are easy to find. It is important to make sure the crib is safe. The bars should be not more than 2³/₈ inches apart.

Legal Fatherhood

One in every 15 men fathers a child while he is a teenager. Yet only about one-third of teen fathers marry the mother of the child. This makes parenting a difficult job. Most teen mothers are single parents. Some teen fathers, however, are becoming more involved in their child's life.

When teens are not married, a child is born without a legal father. Paternity must be established for the child to have a legal dad. Some parents can establish paternity at the hospital. Both parents must sign the Recognition of Parentage (or Declaration of Parentage) form. This form legally establishes paternity.

Children who have legal fathers have many benefits. Fathers can teach their children important things. Children also have the right to receive child support. The parent who does not have custody of the baby usually pays child support. Fathers who pay child support help provide for their children. Fathers who responsibly support their children help reduce the risk that the children will live in poverty.

School or Job Training

Teen parents can work together to raise a child as each balances work and school. Teens who finish high school have many advantages. They are more likely to get a better job than they would without finishing.

Some teens choose to get job training or go to college. Parents need to have skills or training to get a good job. Good jobs pay a living wage. They also provide health insurance and time off for sickness or family emergencies.

A child benefits from having a legal father.

- The child gets help from child support payments.
- The child knows the medical history of his or her father.
- The child may receive Social Security, military, health care, or inheritance benefits.

A father benefits from being a legal father.

- He can see the child's school and medical records.
- He can ask the court for visitation rights.
- He has the right to ask the court for custody of the child.

Affordable Child Care

When teens go to school or to work, they must leave their child with a child care provider. Many teen parents worry about finding good child care. It is hard for parents to leave their child with someone they don't know. Sometimes adult parents may help care for the teens' baby. Finding safe, affordable day care can be stressful for teen parents.

Parenting can be hard at any age. It is especially important for teen parents to seek support and work together.

Points to Consider

How can a teen parent build a healthy attachment with a baby?

What are some ways a teen could afford inexpensive furniture or clothing for a new baby?

Do you think unmarried teens need to identify the legal father? Why or why not?

Chapter Overview

Few teens choose to place their children for adoption.

Independent adoptions allow the birth parents or birth mother to choose the adoptive family. Most services and expenses are free to the birth mother.

Agency adoptions may have more restrictions for the birth mother.

Unmarried birth fathers have no legal rights regarding adoption unless they establish paternity. Only then can they be involved legally in the decision-making process.

Chapter 4

What to Expect if You Choose Adoption

Teen mothers can legally place their children for adoption in 46 states and the District of Columbia. They can do this without the permission of their parents. Yet few teen mothers choose adoption. In fact, less than 10 percent of babies born to teens are placed in adoptive homes.

Many emotional factors affect the decision. Women who are pregnant for nine months feel connected to the baby. They have felt the baby move and kick. Teens who choose adoption believe the benefits outweigh what they can provide as parents at such a young age.

Adoption is not final until after the baby is born. A birth mother must sign a Consent to Adoption form after the birth. Once it is legal, the mother cannot change her mind.

My home life is totally screwed up. I have Alisha, Age 16 lived with my mom, my dad, my grandma, and some other friends. My dad was just released from prison. He showed up drunk and started yelling. I left after he passed out.

I'm living at a safe house for teens now. I decided not to tell my parents about my pregnancy. My counselor has been a great listener. She never tells me what to do. She really lets me work things out in my head. I told her I wanted to place my baby for adoption. I know I can't give my baby what it needs. I'm still learning to take care of myself.

The other girls think I'm nuts. They can't believe I'm going to carry a baby for nine months and let someone else raise it. But I know I'm doing the right thing. I'm going to help choose the parents. I'm going to find a good home where my baby has a chance. I know I'm doing the best thing for my baby.

Independent Adoptions

There are two types of adoptions—independent or agency adoptions. An independent adoption is sometimes called a private adoption. It allows the adoptive parents and birth parents to plan their own adoption. They do not have to follow any rules or policies as they make their plan.

The birth parents choose who they want to adopt their child. When a pregnant teen is unmarried, she makes the legal decision. She also can choose to have an open adoption. This is a type of independent adoption. It allows her and the adoptive parents to know something about one another. This can happen through letters, interviews, or face-to-face meetings with the adoptive family.

The baby goes to the adoptive family right from the hospital in an independent adoption. The birth mother gives the legal rights to her child directly to the adoptive parents. This guarantees that the family she has chosen become the adoptive parents.

Independent adoptions allow the adoptive family to pay certain expenses. All medical and social services are free to the birth mother. Many adoptive parents also pay the legal fees for a birth mother. Many birth mothers choose to attend counseling to help deal with the adoption. Adoptive parents also can pay for counseling expenses for the birth mother.

Teens who choose independent adoption like knowing who the adoptive family will be. This provides comfort and a sense of well-being to the birth mothers. It may help them cope with the decision to place a child for adoption.

Agency Adoptions

In agency adoptions, the agency receives the legal rights to the child from the birth parents. This means the birth mother does not always choose which family adopts her baby. Often a social worker decides the best place for the baby.

A teen mother has these legal rights during an adoption process:

- The right to be represented by an attorney
- The right to receive counseling about adoption plans
- The right to change her mind about the adoption until a certain point
- The first right to parent the child

When my girlfriend and I got pregnant, I Anthony, Age 20 couldn't handle it. I know it wasn't fair to leave her alone. She had to do all the work, but I wasn't ready to be a dad. I told her I didn't care what she chose to do about the pregnancy. It was her decision.

I don't feel that way anymore. I helped make that baby. It took me two years to figure that out. I finally found out where she was living and went to see her. She was going to college and working. She told me she placed our baby for adoption. I couldn't believe it. No one even let me know.

My uncle, who is a lawyer, said I never tried to be declared the legal father. He said I basically gave up my rights by doing nothing. I know I checked out during the pregnancy. But it seems wrong that the father has no rights. I should have done something. I should have taken some responsibility.

Birth mothers can only receive money for counseling services from the adoptive family in an agency adoption. The law limits this. However, the agency may provide other financial support to the birth mother. Agencies may provide open or confidential adoptions for the birth mother. In a confidential adoption, the adoptive parents receive only necessary information. For example, they might receive medical information about the birth parents that would help them care for the child.

Some agencies require that a new baby go into foster care immediately after the birth. The birth mother must first sign the Consent to Adoption form. Then the baby is placed in an adoptive home.

Birth Fathers

Most adoption agencies suggest involving the birth father. This is required if the father is married to the birth mother. It is also required if he is declared the legal father. A birth father may not agree to the adoption. In that case, he must take legal action to be declared the father. He must do this within a certain amount of time after the birth or placement of the baby. Otherwise, he has no rights after that time.

Points to Consider

What are the benefits of an independent adoption?

Why might a teen choose an agency adoption rather than an independent adoption?

Describe the benefits to a child who is placed in an adoptive family.

Chapter Overview

About one in three teen pregnancies end in abortion.

Many states have laws that require that adult parents be informed about a teen's request for an abortion.

Teens receive counseling about all their options at a clinic that provides abortions.

Teens experience many emotions after an abortion.

Chapter 5

What to Expect if You Choose Abortion

Most people have an opinion about abortion. They also have an opinion about the kind of people who have an abortion. In fact, women of all different backgrounds have abortions. Some estimates show that nearly half of all women will have had an abortion by age 45.

Parents in Canada do not have to be notified when a teen chooses an abortion. More than half the U.S. states, however, require that parents be informed when a teen seeks an abortion. It can be a hard decision for a teen to share a pregnancy with an adult. Abortion is the second most common choice for pregnant teens. About one in three teen pregnancies end in abortion in both the United States and Canada.

Teens choose abortion for three main reasons. First, they are concerned about how a baby would change their lives. Second, many teens feel they are not ready or mature enough to have a child. Finally, they are concerned about having enough money to raise a child.

I was about seven weeks pregnant when I decided to have an abortion. My boyfriend said he would support my decision.

Margaret, Age 18

When I was in seventh grade, I wrote a paper about abortion. I believed it was wrong. It seems so long ago that I wrote that. I see things differently now. I am thankful I have a choice.

I'm not ready to be a parent. I've already set up an appointment with my doctor to have a birth control shot. My boyfriend and I have talked a lot more about sexual responsibility. Right now we are choosing not to have sex. I don't know what our future holds. But I do know I have to be prepared.

Most abortions (89 percent) are obtained in the first trimester of pregnancy. In fact, over half of all abortions are obtained within the first 8 weeks. Less than 1 percent occur after 21 weeks. Of these, almost all are done before 23 weeks.

Making the Decision

Choosing abortion can be a tough decision. Teens can talk with their family, friends, and partner about the best decision. They also can talk about choices with a counselor at a clinic that provides abortions. The counselors are specially trained to help a teen make the right decision for her. The Ministry of Health in Canada keeps abortion information confidential.

A surgical abortion is a low-risk procedure that should be done as early as possible. It is important to decide about abortion early in the pregnancy. Medical abortions using pills can be done only until the seventh week of pregnancy. A surgical abortion can be performed up to 15 weeks after the start of the last menstrual period. The number of weeks depends on the state where a woman lives. In Canada, the number of weeks depends on the clinic or hospital providing the abortion. After 15 weeks, the health risks of abortion increase.

Before the Abortion

Once a teen decides to have an abortion, she has a physical exam and tests. A blood or urine test confirms the pregnancy. She receives blood tests. The nurse writes down the individual's medical history. The teen may be tested for STDs, depending on her history. Her weight, temperature, and blood pressure are recorded.

A teen seeking an abortion must sign a form requesting the procedure. The form shows that three things have been done. First, the teen has been informed of all the options. Second, the teen has been counseled about the procedure, its risks, and self-care. Finally, the teen has chosen abortion of her own free will.

The Abortion Procedure

The most common form of abortion is the surgical abortion, or vacuum aspiration. A physician opens a woman's cervix, or opening to the uterus. The doctor removes the contents of the uterus. This is a standard procedure that takes only about 5 to 10 minutes. The woman can go home the same day.

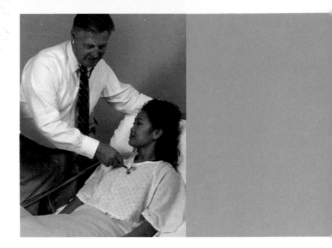

Most women rest for about an hour after the abortion in a supervised recovery area. It is best to have someone else drive the woman home. The clinic provides written instructions for self-care after an abortion. It also provides an emergency phone number if any problems arise.

Recovery After an Abortion

Teens may experience a heavy menstrual period after the abortion. It can last up to 10 days. Some women pass heavy clots of blood. Some may have little or no bleeding. It is recommended that women use pads, not tampons, for any bleeding.

Doctors recommend teens abstain from sex until after the follow-up exam. This usually occurs about three weeks after the bleeding stops. Abstaining from sexual intercourse gives the cervix time to heal. It also protects against infection.

Pregnancy is possible within two weeks after an abortion if a teen doesn't abstain from intercourse. Therefore, it is important to think about prevention. Some teens choose to abstain from intercourse. Others begin using some method of birth control. These choices help prevent future unplanned pregnancies.

The Emotional Effects of Abortion

Women feel many emotions after an abortion. Most commonly, they feel relief and are sure they made the right decision for themselves. Most are sure they made the most responsible decision.

An abrupt hormonal change occurs after any pregnancy, no matter how it ended. As a result of this change, some women feel short-term anger, guilt, regret, or sadness. This is normal. These feelings usually pass quickly.

Teens who experience depression for more than six weeks should seek counseling. The abortion provider may offer ongoing counseling and care to teens.

Teens seek abortions for many reasons. The choice is based on many beliefs and life experiences. Some teens who choose abortion may have to deal with people who are against it. It will help teens to think about how they will react to those who don't agree with their choice.

Points to Consider

Why do you think there are laws that require parents be notified when a teen requests an abortion?

What would happen if abortion were illegal?

How do abortion counselors prepare a teen for an abortion procedure?

What do you think a teen should do about pregnancy prevention after an abortion has been completed?

Chapter Overview

Teens who experience an unplanned pregnancy have three options: abortion, parenthood, or adoption.

Pregnant teens can seek out support when making a decision. If possible, this should include the father of the baby.

Teens must answer tough questions such as whether they are able to make sacrifices.

A careful decision-making process helps to make the best decision.

Chapter 6

Making the Best Decision for You

Teens who are pregnant have a lot to consider. An unplanned pregnancy changes life in every way. Pregnant teens have options. They have the right to choose the best option for them. A thoughtful decision-making process helps to make the best choice.

A teen has to make a decision once a hospital or clinic has confirmed the pregnancy. Teens have three options with an unplanned pregnancy—abortion, parenthood, or adoption.

Seven in ten teen mothers complete high school, but they are less likely to go on to college than women who delay childbearing.

Choosing Abortion

A teen who chooses abortion must make the choice quickly. Teens who choose abortion understand it is a safe procedure if done early in the pregnancy. Some teens, however, may wait too long to make a decision. Teens who put off making a decision may eliminate the option of abortion.

Choosing Parenthood

Teen mothers who choose parenthood must answer some tough questions.

• Am I willing to make sacrifices for my child?

• Do I have the skills to be a good parent?

• Can I provide money and a safe place to raise the baby?

• Will the father of my baby choose to play an active role?

• Am I prepared to be a single parent if the father doesn't choose to be involved?

• Do I have the support of my family and friends?

Teens who choose to parent face some difficulties. Many adults who choose to parent face some of these same challenges.

Choosing Adoption

Some teens may not choose adoption until after the birth of their baby. They may choose to continue the pregnancy while considering adoption.

For a teen who chooses adoption, the idea of being separated from her baby may be painful. Yet she realizes an adoptive family may have much to offer her child.

It is important to include the father in decisions about adoption. Fathers also struggle with decisions about an unplanned pregnancy. Legal fathers can have the right to refuse an adoption.

Fifty-one percent of teens believe that if they were involved in a pregnancy, they would marry the mother or father. In fact, 81 percent of births among teens happen to unmarried teens.

Billy is really popular. I felt so lucky when **Patty, Age 15** he asked me to homecoming. He was everything I could imagine. But I never imagined I would get pregnant. At first, I was really scared. Billy seemed more angry than scared. He started dating a different girl within a week after I told him.

I was so angry. I used the pregnancy to get his attention. I knew he didn't want anybody to know about it. We started dating again, but it wasn't the same.

It took me a while to understand he didn't care for me anymore. By then I was six months pregnant and feeling really alone. I hadn't stopped to think about being a parent. I had only thought about getting Billy to love me.

I've been seeing a counselor. She has helped me look at myself and how I act. Billy and I are actually getting along a lot better. We're talking about placing the baby for adoption. I know I'm not ready to parent. I'm still trying to take care of myself.

Seeking Support

The decision about a pregnancy is hard to make alone. It is true that a woman carries the fetus alone. Yet she did not become pregnant alone. If possible, the father should be included in the decision-making process. He may be able to provide support and guidance. He needs to make decisions about his role in the pregnancy and possible birth.

Family and friends are another source of support. Finding a trusted adult to talk with is an important step. Adults have struggled with similar issues. Often they can listen and help to find good resources and information for the decision. On the other hand, friends may offer an honest opinion. They know what their friends can handle. They offer a different perspective.

Health care clinics and other agencies can provide counseling services. Counselors in these places can give accurate information to help in making the decision. They are objective and can provide another outlook.

Avoiding the Wrong Decision

Unplanned pregnancies stir up strong emotions. Sometimes these feelings can cloud the thinking process. A pregnant teen may have unrealistic thoughts about her partner. She may believe a pregnancy will keep him around. She may think he will marry her. Using a pregnancy to keep a boyfriend is unwise. It is not in the best interest of a child.

Some teens may feel pressured to make a certain decision. For example, a parent may push a daughter toward adoption. Pregnant teens have the right to choose the best option for themselves.

Making the Best Decision

A careful decision-making process can help in making the best choice. Here is an example of such a process:

1. Identify the problem or issue.

2. Gather information about the problem and its possible risks.

3. Define the options.

4. Consider the long-term and short-term outcomes of each option, both positive and negative.

5. Make a decision.

6. Analyze the decision for future learning.

Researchers do not know how many teenage boys become fathers each year. Many women do not include information about the age of the father on the birth certificate.

The decision about teen pregnancy is based on what is happening in a person's present life. It is also based on what may happen in the future. It is important to consider what is best for the child. Teens who choose to parent should have a clear idea about what parenting involves. They need to consider the choice with which they will be most comfortable. Teens must answer some tough questions. Teen parents who go through a strong decision-making process feel better about their decision.

Points to Consider

Why is it important to include the father in decisions about an unplanned pregnancy?

How is not making a decision a kind of decision?

List some tough questions a pregnant teen should ask herself (and her partner) when making a decision.

How can an adult provide support in this decision-making process?

Chapter Overview

It is important for sexually active teens to decide how to prevent pregnancy and disease.

A doctor, nurse, or other health care provider can educate teens about birth control options. Many resources provide accurate information about pregnancy prevention methods.

Teens who choose to be sexually active should talk with their partners about pregnancy prevention. They can discuss together how they can take responsibility.

Chapter 7

Methods to Prevent Pregnancy

Teens who don't use a pregnancy prevention method have a 90 percent chance of pregnancy within a year after first intercourse. Teens who become pregnant once are at risk for a second pregnancy. In the United States, about 25 percent of teen mothers have a second child within two years after the first birth. Therefore, it is important for teens make a plan to deal with future sexual activity.

Avoiding Drugs

Many unplanned pregnancies result from having sex while drunk or on drugs. Being under the influence of alcohol and other drugs makes it difficult to think clearly. Then teens may not be prepared to protect themselves during sex. They may not have protection such as condoms and spermicides. They may not even remember having sex. Not using drugs is one way to help ensure responsible sexual behavior.

Choosing Abstinence

Abstinence is choosing not to have sexual intercourse. It is also choosing not to have oral-genital and genital-to-genital contact. Abstinence is an effective way not to get pregnant. Abstinence is also a way to avoid getting an STD. It costs nothing. Some teens who have already had sex choose to be abstinent in the future.

Choosing Effective Pregnancy Prevention Methods

Sexually active teens must decide which type of pregnancy prevention or birth control works for them. Some types need to be put in place every time a person has sex. Other types offer long-term protection. It is important to use any method consistently and correctly.

I started having sex when I was 14. I
never used any kind of protection. I
wasn't worried about getting anyone pregnant. I just wasn't
thinking about anything, especially the possible consequences.

Malcolm, Age 17

Last year my girlfriend told me she was pregnant. I was forced
to face the consequences.

She talked a lot with her aunt and her mother. She wanted to
have an abortion and asked how I felt about it. I couldn't
imagine doing that. Then I told my dad what happened even
though he and I never talk much. He talked to me about being
ready to parent. He asked how committed I was to my
girlfriend. I saw how I wasn't ready to parent.

My dad and I talk a lot more than we used to. He came with
me and my girlfriend when she ended the pregnancy. None of
my friends believe me, but I haven't had sex . . . well,
intercourse . . . since that happened. I don't want to go through
that again. I've got some growing up to do.

A doctor, nurse, or health educator can provide information about preventing pregnancy and STDs. Many types of pregnancy prevention methods are available. Teens must consider their own behaviors before choosing the best method for them.

Where to Find Pregnancy Prevention Methods

Some pregnancy prevention methods can be purchased at stores without a prescription. A written order from a doctor is not needed to buy them. Such methods include condoms and spermicides. These are called over-the-counter contraceptives. Condoms are the most common over-the-counter method of pregnancy prevention. Anyone is legally able to purchase over-the-counter methods.

Other pregnancy prevention methods require a prescription. A woman must get the prescription and instructions at a clinic or hospital. Usually she must have a physical examination in order to receive the prescription. Such methods include birth control pills, emergency contraceptive pills, progestin, and a diaphragm. Progestin is commonly called "the shot." It is given to a woman through a shot, pills, or an implant under the skin.

Pregnancy Prevention Options

Nonprescription

1 Male condom—A thin latex or polyurethane covering that fits over the penis to catch sperm. Most effective when used with a spermicide. Also protects against sexually transmitted diseases.

2 Female condom—A bag-like piece of polyurethane that fits inside the vagina. Helps to prevent pregnancy by keeping sperm out of the uterus. Also protects against sexually transmitted diseases.

3 Spermicide—A foam, cream, tablet, or gel put into the vagina to kill sperm. When used correctly together, condoms and spermicides are 97 percent effective in preventing pregnancy.

Prescription

1 Birth control pills—A daily pill that prevents an egg from being released each month.

2 Progestin—A drug given to a woman to prevent an egg from being released each month. Progestin can be given in the form of pills, as a shot, or implanted under the skin.

3 Emergency contraceptive pill (morning after pill)—A combination of tablets that provides emergency birth control when used immediately after unprotected sex or within 72 hours. This is not meant to be an ongoing birth control method. It will not work if implantation of the fertilized egg has occurred.

4 Diaphragm—A rubber cup placed over the cervix to keep sperm out of the uterus. Must be used with a spermicide and a male condom.

Over three-fourths of teenagers use some contraceptive method the first time they have intercourse.

The contraceptive teens use most frequently is the condom (66 percent). Teens are next most likely to use birth control pills (40 percent). One in three teen females who use the pill also use the condom.

Partners Should Talk

Most importantly, partners need to talk honestly about sex and birth control. Teens who choose to be sexually active need to discuss pregnancy prevention options with their partner. Such discussion helps the couple share the responsibility. It is also important to discuss what would happen if the woman becomes pregnant. Honest communication can help a couple make healthy choices.

Points to Consider

Why should the male use a condom if the female is already using birth control pills or the shot?

Which birth control method do you think is best for sexually active teens? Explain your answer.

Do you think a teen could use birth control pills effectively? Why or why not?

How would you encourage a teen couple to talk more about birth control methods and sexual choices?

Chapter Overview

Teens can develop a plan to build a healthy future. Such a plan includes a good support system and making healthy decisions about their life.

Teens who commit to finishing school or job training create a higher standard of living for themselves.

Before starting a sexual relationship, teens can communicate with their partners about sexual boundaries and pregnancy prevention methods.

It is important to make a commitment to parenting.

Chapter 8

Your Future—
Making It Work for You

Make a Plan

It helps to make a plan in order to build a healthy future. The plan can include short-term and long-term goals. It includes figuring out what to do now to reach those goals. A plan for the future might include some of the following actions.

1. Surround Yourself With Good People

A pregnancy can cause teens to reevaluate the people in their life. Support and honesty are important foundations for friendship. Teens can look for friends who promote a healthy lifestyle. They may not want friends who pressure them to do things they don't want to do. Choosing healthy friends helps to achieve goals.

My pregnancy was a wake-up call. I had **Anneeta, Age 18** dropped out of school and was partying a lot. I had tried to work but never kept a job very long. I couldn't handle my supervisors telling me what to do.

I didn't even know who the father was. Sometimes I would drink so much I would black out. I don't even like sex that much. Somehow I kept ending up having it anyway.

I decided right away to get an abortion. The counselor at the clinic was so honest with me. She told me I was at high risk for HIV, STDs, and more pregnancies. She referred me to a safe house and a counselor.

After the abortion, I checked myself into the safe house. I'm learning how to stay clean. I've also started making new friends. They make me laugh. We do stuff I've never done before. And it's safe. I'm attending school part time. It's been really hard at times, but I feel good about where I'm going. At least now I can see where I'm going. And I like it.

2. Value Your Education

Education should come first. Teens have many choices for schools and types of training. Some schools provide vocational or job training. Alternative learning centers have small classes and flexible schedules. The benefits of having education outweigh the struggles that result from not having education.

3. Practice for Future Parenting

Most people will parent at some point in their life even if they choose not to have children. Whenever people take time to work and play with a child, they are parenting. A teen who becomes an uncle or an aunt has a chance to practice parenting a child. Baby-sitting or volunteering to work with children are ways teens can practice for future parenting.

4. Communicate

Teens who choose to be sexually active risk pregnancy. Couples need to talk about this choice. They need to agree on a pregnancy prevention method. Couples also need to set clear boundaries around sexual behavior. Teens who talk about their sexual boundaries build a healthy relationship.

5. Imagine Your Partner Being a Parent

Few teens think of sexual intercourse in relationship to possible parenting. Teens need to ask themselves if their partner is parent material. They need to ask whether they want a relationship with that person for the rest of their child's life. Teens may choose not to have sex with their partner based on their honest answers to these questions.

6. Make Healthy Choices

Teens can make healthy decisions and choices when they understand themselves. When they know their limitations, they can avoid certain situations.

7. Focus on Self-Improvement

Teens who like themselves find that other people admire and like them. Teens learn to like themselves by giving themselves positive messages every day. They learn to be confident of the healthy choices they make. The choices may not be popular, but they may be in an individual's best interests.

8. Take Responsibility for Your Actions

If you choose to be sexually active, you can be responsible by having protected sex. Postponing sexual activity until you're older is also a way to be sexually responsible. Sexual responsibility means respecting your partner's limits and communicating with him or her. It means never forcing sex on another person.

If You Have to Make a Decision Now . . .

Teens have to make tough decisions every day. Yet dealing with an unplanned pregnancy is a life-changing decision. Using the decision-making process on page 42 can help. It's important to consider all the options and gather information. Then you can make the best decision for you.

Things teens can do to prepare for future parenting:

1. Baby-sit or volunteer to work with children.
2. Play with kids in the neighborhood.
3. Volunteer to mentor or tutor a younger child.
4. Take a parenting or family living class at school.
5. Talk to good parents. Find out what it takes to be a good parent.
6. Finish school to increase chances of finding a well-paying job.

If you choose to parent, make a commitment to it. Take parenting classes. Read and learn as much as possible about child development. Work to complete school or job training so you can help support your family. Finally, try to work with your partner so your child has a chance to know both parents.

What are two short-term and two long-term goals you would include in your plan for the future?

What do you think is the best method to prevent a second pregnancy?

What do you think could help reduce the number of teen pregnancies in the United States and Canada?

Name three commitments that would help teens if they choose to parent.

Glossary

abortion (uh-BOR-shuhn)—a procedure that ends a pregnancy

abstinence (AB-stuh-nenss)—the willful avoidance of something; choosing not to have sexual relations.

adoption (uh-DOP-shuhn)—the process in which adults take the child of other parents into their family and become the legal parents

birth parents (BURTH PAIR-uhntss)—the mother and father to whom a child is born

cervix (sur-VIKS)—the narrow outer opening to the uterus

child support (CHILDE suh-PORT)—money that the parent without custody pays to support a child

contraceptive (kon-truh-SEP-tiv)—something that prevents conception; a birth control pill is a contraceptive.

egg (EG)—the female reproductive cell; when fertilized by male sperm, it develops into a new human being.

fetus (FEE-tuhss)—an unborn, developing human being

hormone (HOR-mohn)—a chemical that controls a body function

menstruation (men-stroo-AY-shuhn)—the monthly release of the lining of the uterus

paternity (puh-TUR-nuh-tee)—being a father

prenatal care (pree-NAY-tuhl KAIR)—a pregnant woman's regular doctor visits before a baby is born

sexual intercourse (SEK-shoo-uhl IN-tur-korss)—penetration of the penis into the vagina

sperm (SPURM)—the male reproductive cell; a sperm is capable of fertilizing a female's egg.

For More Information

Arthur, Shirley M., and Jeanne W. Lindsay. *Surviving Teen Pregnancy: Your Choices, Dreams, Decisions.* Buena Park, CA: Morning Glory Press, 1996.

Barr, Linda, and Catherine Monserrat. *Teenage Pregnancy: A New Beginning.* Albuquerque, NM: New Futures, 1996.

Eisenberg, Arlene, Heidi Eisenberg Murkoff, and Sandee Eisenberg Hathaway. *What to Expect When You're Expecting.* New York: Workman, 1996.

Endersbe, Julie K. *Teen Fathers: Getting Involved.* Mankato, MN: Capstone Press, 2000.

Endersbe, Julie K. *Teen Mothers: Raising a Baby.* Mankato, MN: Capstone Press, 2000.

Useful Addresses and Internet Sites

National Abortion Federation
1755 Massachusetts Avenue NW, Suite 600
Washington, DC 20036

National Adoption Information Clearinghouse
(NAIC)
11426 Rockville Pike, Suite 410
Rockville, MD 20852

National Campaign to Prevent Teen Pregnancy
2100 M Street NW, Suite 300
Washington, DC 20037
www.teenpregnancy.org

Planned Parenthood Federation of America
810 Seventh Avenue
New York, NY 10019
1-800-230-7526
www.plannedparenthood.org

Planned Parenthood Federation of Canada
1 Nicholas Street, Suite 430
Ottawa, ON K1N 7B7
CANADA
www.ppfc.ca

Adoption Council of Canada
www.adoption.ca
Umbrella organization for adoption in Canada

AdoptioNetwork
www.adoption.org/bparents
Information for a woman considering adoption
for her baby

Advocates for Youth
www.advocatesforyouth.org
Information for teens on preventing HIV, teen
pregnancy, and more

Canadian Abortion Rights Action League
www.caral.ca
Provides information about abortion in Canada

teenwire
www.teenwire.com
Sexuality and relationship information for
teens

Index

abortion, 6, 29–34, 38, 47, 54
    emotional effects of, 34
    procedure, 32–33
    reasons for, 30
    recovery from, 33
abstinence, 33, 46
adoption, 6, 23–27, 39
    agency, 25–27
    father's rights and, 27
    independent, 24–25
agency adoptions, 25
alcohol, 46, 54
attachment, 17, 18

baby care, 18–19
birth control pills, 7, 48, 49, 50
birth control shot, 30

cesarean births, 14–15
childbirth, 14–15
    classes, 15, 18
child care, 21
child development, 14, 58
child support, 20
commitment, 58
communication, 50, 56
condoms, 5, 7, 46, 48, 49, 50
confidence, 57
confidential adoptions, 27
Consent to Adoption, 23, 27
contraceptives, 8, 33, 45–50
contractions, 14
counselors, 24, 25, 27, 31, 34, 40,
    41, 54

cribs, 19
custody, 20

day care. *See* child care
decisions, 6, 11, 37–43
    about abortion, 29–34, 38
    about adoption, 23–27, 39
    about parenting, 17–21, 38–39
    avoiding the wrong, 42
    making the best, 42–43
Declaration of Parentage, 20
diaphragm, 49
drugs, 46

education, 20, 38, 55, 58
emergency contraceptive pill, 48, 49
emotions, 5, 23, 34, 42, 57
expenses, 19

families, telling, 11, 41
fathers
    and decision-making process, 39, 41
    importance of, 20
    legal, 19–21, 27, 39
    responsibilities of, 7, 26
feeding, 18
feelings. *See* emotions
foster care, 27
friendships, 41, 53

health insurance, 19, 20
honesty, 50, 53, 56
hormones, 6, 34